Benjamin Elliott

Spectres on the Landscape

Hauntological Poems of Lament, Folklore and the Macabre

Introduction

Have you ever awoken in the night with a distinct sense of fear, and yet, no reason can be found as to why? Have you ever walked through the woods alone and felt that creeping tingle at the base of your neck, almost as if someone is watching you? Have you ever looked up and listened to the hum of electrical pylons, and been filled with an overwhelming dread? Or, perhaps you've seen something at the corner of your eye dart into the shadows. If so, then these poems might just be up your street.

I have often wondered what it was, even as a small boy, that caused me to fear the dark corners of my bedroom, or the silent and still remoteness of the landing at the top of the stairs, and the autumnal walks in the countryside. It's perfectly plausible to consider that this all stems from some evolutionary trait hardwired into us, demonstrating some form of self-preservation and an aversion to the danger of the 'unknown'. But this seems all to easy an explanation, and ultimately strips the fun out of the subject. After all, what would the darkness be without monsters? Extremely boring I would imagine.

And in this we can begin to understand the fireside stories of our forebears, who, after a long day of hunting and farming would return to the community with strange tales of Banshees and the Green Man. Figures that stalk the hills and valleys waiting for an unsuspecting onlooker to catch a glance of something they shouldn't have seen and fall foul of its ancient power.

Folklore and horror are often intricately linked, and anyone who is familiar with the stories of M.R James or Charles Dickens will know all too well the compelling power one can create when you combine cultural traditions of story-telling with the spice of the macabre. We love to be frightened. When we move away from the idea that horror, for the purposes of entertainment, is not so much about someone coming to a sticky end but more about the chill of the night, the rustle of something that may or may not be outside the tent when you go camping, or the creak of a floorboard, you can begin to see that real fear, real horror, can be found in the simplest and smallest of places, amplified by the worst enemy of all, our imagination. Here we can begin to grasp the reality, that there is nothing to grasp! And that is real horror.

Of course, Folkish tales aren't exclusively macabre or horrifying, they can also have a lamentable quality. A lament, like so many complex human emotions, can also have a raw unchained beauty to it, like 'Tristan and Isolde' or 'Tannhauser'. Just take Emily Brontë's work 'Wuthering Heights'. She expertly crafted a deep, brooding vision of passionate love, underpinned with ancient tragedy, all set on the Yorkshire Moors, combining the internal reality of our emotions, set against a bleak yet beautiful natural landscape. The bottomless caverns of the human heart, imagination, and wistful longing are well documented, and illustrate to us that we humble humans have been trying to articulate so much of what makes us who we are, for so long, that we have almost mastered its art. In James Hilton's 'Lost Horizon', we see more of this mysterious quality, a world of antique treasures, and dark secrets. An ever present reminder that at the heart of all human matters is a thirst to understand what cannot be understood.

I think it is perfectly obvious that the dark and macabre nature of things, the horrifying, is not necessarily about the bogyman who lives 'under the stairs'. That's just an allegory, a means of manifesting what cannot be seen, only felt. More than this, it's about the darker corners of our hearts, and what they project into the world. Folklore, and lamentable tales play into that idea, an idea that we can enrich the physical world around us with our own emotions.

In an attempt to locate that intricate place where the dark, warm, undulating breath lies, was easier than I thought it would be. And I say warm, because I feel that at the core of such folkish lamentations and dark imagery is a womb like pool of inspiration, a sacred place reserved just for us, a place that springs forth all those collective ideas that rest beneath the surface of us all. In many ways, our universal inheritance. What certainly jumped out at me, was how easy some of the prose came, and how deep the well of narratives was. It was as if decades and decades of inspiration had been left untouched, just waiting to be disturbed. Laying, just under the surface, breathing, waiting.

And it's on days, such as these, when the light begins to fade, and the summer has sung its last, and autumn's leafy gown descends upon us all, that we start to feel that great pull back into the embrace of nature. It's the sadness of a passing year, the gentle drift from life into death that generates, at least in me, the greatest of inspiration. It's not that summer doesn't have its charm, but its just too happy, too polished. The darker months give us shadows. Shadows that expose the cracks, the corners, the thought that someone might be following you home on a foggy night. Things become spooky.

I think you can begin to see where I'm coming from.

In this new collection of poems, you may notice the odd one here and there that has slipped in from one of my other works. That's because they simply screamed like a Banshee to be included. Their conception might actually have been pulled from the same well of inspiration, possibly slipping through the cracks of my imagination without me noticing, and as such I wanted to give them the chance to be part of a different narrative, a chance to dance to a slightly different tune. As for everything else, it's all new!

I've spent many an afternoon and evening scaring myself to death in an attempt to create what I feel is an accurate, and dare I say it, noble attempt and this genre. Believe me when I say, the creaks and groans of the house got louder each night I committed myself to work on a new poem, which only fueled my desire to write, even more.

Even as I sit here writing at my old library table, I'm looking around my living and dining room. The Afghan rugs on the floor, the bookcase behind me, and the piano, cluttered with archaeological finds and obscure neolithic sculptures all covered in dust, and a shadow has descended over me. Not in a wicked way, but in a whimsical sense. Those notions of folklore and lament, underpinned by the darkness, are more alive than ever, and are part of not just my life, but all of our lives. We all rest in a tiny pocket of time, a tiny little space where stories, experiences, and emotions come together and draw us into another world, another world where things aren't always as they seem, and where our imagination of the past is as real as the way we perceive it when we finally decide to turn the lights out, and try to get some sleep…

In the course of bringing this work together I've explored a whole host of different philosophical and historical narratives, and found that these notions that I seek to capture are part of a far wider scope of human thought and philosophical understanding. Hauntology, for example, a portmanteau of 'haunting' and 'ontology', (a philosophical concept developed by the French philosopher Jacques Derrida) is the study of spectralities, an array of concepts referring to the persistence of elements from our social and cultural past, and focuses on the notion that ghosts aren't necessarily ghoulish apparitions that float around old houses in the country, but are actually the physical and philosophical remnants of the past that still exist in our present world today, affecting us emotionally and physically. A great example would be an abandoned factory from the 60's, electrical pylons from the 70's, or the obsolete ideological frame work of European communism, a dead world that still 'haunts' the lives of those people who still remember it, an unrealized future that belongs to the past. This concept is far more complex than I have been able to lay out for you here, but it definitely gives a great deal more credence to the contents of this work, demonstrating that there is a legitimate reason to be spooked, and that fear and horror don't exclusively belong to an ancient or far-flung era, but can reside with us in the present, inspired by a past only three or four decades old. It's almost like an incomplete paradigm shift, a new set rules and ideas that still maintain echoes of what was there before, like an itch that can't be scratched. Small and insignificant, yet persistent.

If you take the time to look at hauntological themes, you'll find that there is a whole 'other world' of exploration. A world that demands to be seen and felt. It screams out from the past, forcing you out of neutrality and clean lines, and into a space of perpetual decay.

We often think in this day and age that if we contextualize things, or understand them to a far greater degree, maybe even simplify them, then we have less to be afraid of. I disagree. In many respects, exploring things from different philosophical angles, or different spectral plains, actually makes these types of subjects all the more terrifying, because they demonstrate that although we are able to reach out and touch the physical manifestations of the things that frighten us, there are, and always will be a component that just can't be accessed, existing in a dimension that we as mere mortals, trapped in this bubble of the present, can no longer grasp. And it's in this bubble that I will leave you. Leave you to contemplate your own terrors. Leave you to bask in your own shadows. Leave you at the mercy of the spectres on the landscape

Benjamin J Elliott

This book is dedicated to my grandmother,
Beatrice Anita Groves
*When as a child, I was convinced
she was a witch.*
(1926-2023)

Just a Story

Patriotism is dead, on a long drawn winter day, frayed
Like a shirt sleeve. Yet, it was the only eye to view
The hills, the setting sun, the flint clad walls and inns.
With a whisper of ancient ghosts, the hero, the gods,
All left to die under the fading days.

I am no pride armored fool. Clad in a wash of thin vagaries.
The heavy yolk I bear, is made of a dread cloth, dread,
Made to endure under its weight. Your drapery is crust.
The bell that rings still echoes, but it is just that. An echo.

Where is left here, on green and pleasant lands?
Sold out, chopped up, sealed in corruption. On sale.
A gesture from the sky, rays and swooping flash that flies,
An Ash, solitary among the heavy brow of colored cloud,
And now, nothing more than glass. A sorrow. A fracture.

Who now do we beseech? Deceived by a patriots wicked lie.
Our love so deep and holy, betrayed by falsehood.
It's all we had.
Where now do we dig, in rich soil, on a crest that overlooks
Where once great kings were throned, in honest glory,
Just a story

Lepenski Vir

If currents grant the flow of life,
And whirlpools snag all vine and Pike.
There's no cross here, its religions fall,
In the old God's world, we hear the call.

No fun or joy is found in he,
In this place is the ancient 'we'.
Where spirits and shadows are one in the same,
And no friendly words or songs will tame.

These Gods belong to a bygone time,
When stone and air could shape the sign.
And on the streams did old folk hunt,
With spear in hand on the gravel front.

What ancient wisdom was found in thee,
What manner of life did you give to see.
Carved in stone, and in prominence placed,
Long times to feel the flames you face.

What spectral power did you once own,
In darkened hollows, legend sewn.
Some piscine terror that stalks the stag,
In times lost foggy, wintery crag.

A Wasted Day

The summer days are past, richness failing in the morning sun,
The clouds conspire to push me back into the ground, no elevation.
Where evening settles its head in the passing of the day,
Where the dreams begin,
And on the drifting weight of the cooling night I glance
Towards the window, waiting
For the ghosts of yesterday to save me.

Changing winds and tides change our lives, pushed along
Another road, another end,
Too long it has been, where once I danced and loved, to be left,
Unknowing, and unknown.
Longing now for the touch, the warmth, the embrace of golden curls
Bronzed flesh,
But pushed into darkness, away from her hands, her smile, her eyes.

Once more, like so many times before, I see the leaves falling,
And picked up
By the darkening breeze of lonesome nights, alone,
Resting on thoughts.
The chilling sound of my voice with no response, no tears, and no
Compassion,
I am left, packed away like a bad memory, gathering dust,
A relic on the shelf.

I dream, at night, that I am not alone. And Happy, able to hold
The curves of another,
While outside nature scratches at the window, reminders, the call
Back home.
Pinning back a smile, fixed for now, but drowning me inside.
Grasping, gasping,
A lonely day, cast into the fire. A wasted day, filled with desire…

The Kikimora

Good or bad, I cannot tell,
And on that chance, she casts a spell.
The fated thought you catch a glance,
Shadows of sorts, a spirit's dance.

Scratching at the boards at night,
You tell yourself its mice in flight.
But in the dark you feel her scratch,
The Kikimora turns the latch.

Don't look now, behind the stove,
A child flees, nowhere to go.
She might appear, or stay out of sight,
So upturn a broom, by the door late at night.

Spinning thread, and by extension,
The Kikimora we do not mention.
Disturbing the house, and all within,
To change our ways, and do not sin.

From dusk till dawn, the magician's cat,
Regals with stories, while she spins flax.
But danger lurks in her thoughts so told,
With evil intentions she has for this world.

Dusty rusty griped in fear,
You know she's there, from the sheets you peer.
Waiting up, in the shadows tone,
Griped in the darkness, turned to stone.

He Waits

He waits, his listless lust rumbling, pulling you closer,
Luring you in,
A dream that comes when days begin to fade,
And the silent role of night surrounds you.
Oh, he can wait. His browning crispy smile, and hollow sockets
Watch,
For the trip, the fall, the last gasp before the silent twirling dance
Of death.
Consumed, by the night, his breath catches your neck. You shudder.

His deceiving colours, and wistful rays of fading light,
Temptations. Temptations to sleep.
Temptations to the earth where decay breeds lost loves notions.
Potions of deception,
Drink deep the moistening soil, pulling you closer,
Down to his hands
Where substance beats mislaid rhythms. Under stone and leaf,
Gently, to pull you apart.
Flaked, snapped, and squashed, by feet that forget, and hands
That cannot feel.

Peeling back the flesh, the juicy life that once filled the air is dried
Out, sucked away,
His governing hollow glance that dances over all that lives
For summers song,
Gone, only tortured coasts of silent pebbles,
Rebelling against the tide.
Have you seen him? Opened your senses to feel him on the air.
The smell of change
As fleeting flocked hooves dart for cover. And Gods own orchestras
Flit to the nest.
→

The rites of rotting petal and crow pecked sodden flesh, the end.
Meet him out on the Moors, the Downs, the Dales. He's there,
Waiting for you
To take a stroll, a ramble. Caught for a moment on the breeze,
Your breath is stolen.
And if standing stones in fog did speak, they would say...
"He waits, his listless lust rumbling, pulling you closer,
Luring you in"

A Shoe for a Head

Such footsteps have been heard by others,
But not from jolly or festive lovers.
The starkest choice of darkened corners,
Reserved for lament, and weeping mourners.

Thrust in towards the mind you know,
To secret places, you dare not go.
That place of which is seldom said,
You see the man with a shoe for a head!

A twisted rhyme of near completion,
Stains the mind, an infestation.
Standing at the foot of one's bed,
You see him in your stricken dread.

This thing from deep within the collection,
To speak of it would mean to section.
And should you dare to ask the questions,
Making pains to find connections.

It's too late now, these lines you've seen,
That place in which safety had been.
For now it's time to lose your mind,
Or lose your head, and replace in kind.

Oh pity you the one who's seen,
What should be left in abstract dream.
The mind you wished you had not read,
About the man with a shoe for a head.

The Black Dog

Stalked, wondering creature of omens,
Chosen.
Sussex, Salop, and Suffolk known.
No forewarning, phantom roam.

Noxious odour on a misty stage,
The battle waged.
Heart choked throats, the terror seen.
Lips licked clean.

No solid claim, or clearing mention,
Hesitation.
No, these teeth, grinning at its witness
No sweetness.

No growl or bark, yet stricken horror,
Hark!
Waiting at the end of lanes, crunching tone.
Panic, into clothing fibers,
Sewn.

One moment here, then gone,
And in legend. Where from?
Near the Devil's Nags,
And a terrible wonder wrought.
Vanishes after glowing eyes,
Caught.

Boundaries, fields, graves and gallows,
A lane that narrows.
Watch for the Dog.
Near church and farm,
Distant barn.
Emerge from fog.

The Baba Yaga

Pity them, those long lost children,
Strolled gaily through the glade.
They came to her who is seldom seen,
And there, misfortune made.

That bitter, retched, aged hag,
Who parents warned in stories.
Sharpened claws which clothes will snag,
In lands of faded glories.

In a forest hut that turns forever,
On chicken's feet, you see.
And in those four walls is where she lives,
The Baba Yaga be!

The young ones, oh they're far more tender,
They're the ones she likes the most.
And even though you're safe at home,
Her oven is hot to roast.

In darkened corners, of ancient woods,
That's where her hut is found.
So if you wish to sneak a glance,
Try not to make a sound.

To lose yourself in her domain,
Is a foolish thing to do.
She'll sweep away the paths you trod,
You're hopeless, and without a clue.

The Shadows that Sit in the Hall

I cower. Draped in a cloak of darkness.
Fleeting shift of feet to avoid the touch,
Of those that hang in the air, waiting
For to catch or snatch at my nightly wears.
A cold breeze at your ankles,
A knowing breath on your neck.

Silence is no safety. Not here.
Here is where they dance, on and on and around,
You dart from hall to stairs, carried away by fear,
Ushered like flexed branches in a storm,
Stretched against an unseen force, howling reck.
Stretched the visceral fibers.

There they are. The figures that sit in the hall.
Slouched against the shadows. Watching,
Lolling head the mark of decay.
Reach out, reach before they catch you.
The switch on the left. No, the right! No, No…
Fumbling dumb in the dark. Hands on your shoulders.

Open the door and close it quick. Under the sheets,
Before the hands that grasp the child's foot,
Hurried on.
Sanctity in duvet drowned. But wait, stricken eyes of terror,
And how the dancing grin of night?
Hands reaching from beneath the bed.
You groan in silence…

The Cycle

I am home. Long lost the Father's creed.
We danced around the stones, marked seasons,
Where once the corners were granted light.
A wisdom un-seated.

Club towed, and cauldron fed followers. Setting sun.
We dream of the elements, hue stamped wonders,
Close to home, lost is the queen.
Floral crown, cast to the winds. Blown away.

Pursue the clustered dreams of heather, of the winds.
Ancient oak of leafy nobility. Dreamt up, and forgotten,
In the light that fades as the Gods descend.
Gentle are the faces of water.

Spirited essence that lifts the soul, unhindered.
Richness of earths secrets, unfolded, given up,
No sight for those who cannot see.
Ignorance breeding, long lived lust.

Take me away, on the winds that lead me home.
Fostered and garnered in the womb of the mother,
I have died a thousand times.
Homeward bound. Onward skip the end of summers dance.

Remnants Old Ruin

Feeling lost, inside, alone.
Silent column,
Made from stone.
Crumbling echoes, dusted,
And former faith speakers.
Spiritual seekers.

Lamentable light, cutting through.
Striking empty air,
Dry, pitiable view.
Hastened gust through,
A broken roof,
Skyward, heavens proof.

Corners eye caught.
Fleeting moment,
Fading thought.
Slabs left sandy parched,
No honour here,
A pilgrims tear.

Leaning hands against the alter.
Remnants old ruin,
Glory found faulter.
The architype is torn
Asunder, griefs lost cause,
In decaying vaults…
We pause.

The Cailleach

Up, and aloft,
Black cap,
Not doffed.
Spectral wing, lift,
On farmland, perched, croft

Dark draped, a croaking jest,
Perched up high,
A nest.
Natures dark cleaner,
Carrion's zest.

Fallen stag,
Bones and flesh, left
For the hag.
Winter and storm, the Cailleach,
Left overs. A torn rag.

Twinkling eye,
Laughing cry,
Over there, and here
You spy.
Waiting for death. A Rotten sigh.

That Place.

The shadow of terror, it gripped me,
In a grasp that drew the strength from my heart.
In places where one should feel safe,
I am undone.

The thickening night where once the gentle moth he danced,
It has been reduced to genocide.
And the dusty musty air of death, it looms,
Like the decay of the past rising from the ground.

Ancient cobbles, where feet should tap as one walks,
Now they play host to a phantom in flight.
I have seen this before,
But not here.

The smell of thick murder on the air,
Masked by deception.
I am compelled to the basement, but
What waits for me I already know.

I know this smell, and I know
Who this trio is.
I see the three of them, locked
Together in an embrace. But they are dry and dead.

Now with my waking eyes I understand, it's the story
She told me that evening.
Those dry bones.
Leave it not to me oh lord to breathe
life into them.
Please.

Stalked

There's a lonely trod path,
Or so it is said,
When an unknowing traveler,
Is stalked by the dead.

A clutch at your shoulder,
You turn to look round,
But nothing is present,
Just your breath, and no sound.

You quicken your pace,
On the chance you'll outrun,
Sodden path beneath feet,
And trees block out the sun.

The shadows that fall,
On the path as you flee,
Reaching out to embrace you,
Though the darkness you see.

Shift on the breeze,
Whipped up by your flight,
They grasp at your ankles,
Whisked off in the fight.

The branches turned down,
Over panic struck gloom,
Turn witness to shadows,
Sleepy hallows consume.
→

And it's when you are back,
In the home that you know,
To find you've locked yourself in,
With this horror, alone…

If You Knew Me, Then You Would Know

Pinched. Unknown.
Hooked darts embedded in my skin
From some plant, deviant foliage.
It was a dream, where company was strained
And I, carrying the burden of a hope
Slip into the darkness, hidden amongst the curling bracken.
The moonlit land, it cries for the sun.
The rain, it washes us away.

Solemn Retrospect

This is a shadow, long drawn, stretched out,
Taught!
An empty tomorrow of futures past. The draft
At a broken window, a solemn retrospect.
Their columns are rust, choked fame, acidy
Of the rain is its work.
And here, among the giants, we go,
To visit the humming hill.

Its hand fell upon my shoulder, behind me
It pointed forward, into a blank.
Its hollow stone sockets glare.
Like a lintel poised above, it perches, falsely
Claiming structure.
Mold clad. It casts a shadow.
There was an industry, once,
Holding up a star, fallen now.

A concrete tomb, grinning frenzy.
The silent sigh of clinging ivy,
The sickle cut specter.
Clustered costs and chain,
No future won.
We are haunted by a shadow
Long drawn

The Face at the Window

Livid black the eyes pupil,
A tearing stare of glassy terror,
Framed in a peeling past.
Stricken pulled pulse of decay.
A passing fancy
A peering jest of the devils own.

Fixed to the spot, stone tone haunting,
Corporal punishment of silence.
It watches, tracing the pulse,
Feeling with a gaze, slouched rot.
Haggard sagged energy of sight,
See it blankly access.

It's a stain on the mind, burnt in
Dirt between the gaps that can't be scrubbed.
A flattened flexed picture you hold
To unsee, to brace the minds molds.
Hold. Reading sight the bodies charge.
You are reflected. Wretched.

I Didn't Know, But I Knew...

There is a shape without substance, a haunting reflection of lateral space.
Placed, not grown, on a landscape that is forever possessed.
The time is marked on the charts that make up our lives, but there is no relation.
We are in a bubble, stalked by pasts dread features.
Alone. Relatable lamentations.
I fear the sound. The silent vibrations beneath the surface.

The Ghosts that are awakening.
Where do we go from here? With no future sight. Only past.
Who is this that pulls at the latch? How have I suppressed this fear?
A hat sits on the table. Unworn, no purpose.
A fallen leaf.
The sun shines through a hole in the clouds. Casting itself upon ancient stones.
Home is a memory. Our future is lost to the past.

...And Now, I Know.

The light forms behind a tree, alone
Standing in the bleak darkness.
A freezing fog of sorrow, spent
Days on wind swept hills.
There is a shriek in the shadows, caught
By a gasp of nocturnal spirits.
They are dead images of the fallen, traces
Of a lost world in tatters.

Natures climbing vine and spinning web, creepers
Working their way through crumbling cement.
The owl waits with knowing gaze, held
In silent reclaiming motion.
A curling leaf bathed in moonlight, covering
The distant echoes.
And the moss that clings to the bark, reflects
The light that forms behind a tree, alone

-Other Publications by This Author-

Home by the Sea (Poetic Reflections)

Broken Mirrors (Poetic Fragments)

The Corner of My Eye (Stories and Cautionary Tales)

Lateral Shadows (Poetic Quests)

Design for Life (Novella)

Making Connections

The Passing of the Days (Poetic Wandering)

Talking Colours (Collected Works of Poetry)

The Sun, The Seasons, and The Swastika
(A Guide to One of the World's Oldest Symbols)

Printed in Great Britain
by Amazon

36846480R00030